BOSS BABY C's
The Official Alphabet Book for Young Entrepreneurs

By Patrice Alves
Illustrated by Richard Alves

Copyright 2020 Patrice Alves
ISBN: 978-1-7348157-6-4

All rights reserved. No part of this publication may be reproduced, distributed, or transmitted in any form or by any means, including photocopying,recording, or other electronic or mechanical methods, without prior written permission of the publisher, except in the case of brief quotations embodied in critical reviews and certain other noncommercial uses permitted by copyright law. For permission requests, write to publisher, addressed "Attention: Permissions Coordinator", at the address below.

Any references to historical events, real people, or real places are used fictitiously, names, characters, and places are products of the authors imagination.

First printing edition 2021 in the United States

Unseen Handz Media

www.unseenhandz.com

A LETTER FROM THE AUTHOR

I would like to give an honor to the Most High for blessing me with the knowledge, skill, and ability to create something this powerful! I would also like to thank my nieces and nephews, known as the "Dream Team" for their love and support! Trust the process. To my nephew Richie, this is for you! He captured these visuals at just fifteen! Rich, you are an amazing artist, and the world needs to know and see it. To my young king, Malik, to be a CEO at your age is legendary! Leek, continue to be the man God created you to be! Huge thanks to my partner in everything, Mike, my Unseen Handz team, and all those who believe and inspire me. Remember, a child shall lead them.

B Is for BUSINESS
(/biznes/)

Own what you love to do.

C Is for CREDIT
(/kredet/)

Credit is money that you must pay back.

Use less than 30 percent of your limit to keep your credit on track!

 # Is for ENTREPRENEUR
(/an.tre.pre.noo.er/)

Be your own BOSS!

F Is for FINANCE
(/finans/)

That's when you need help to pay the cost.

 **Is for INVEST**
(/in.vest/)

Pour into what you believe in.

J Is for JOB
(/jab/)

When you work to pay for things you will be needing.

 **Is for KNOW**
(/no/)

The more you know,
the more you grow.

L Is for LOAN
(/lon/)

A loan is money you borrow.

M Is for MONEY

(/mun.ne/)

Save up for tomorrow!

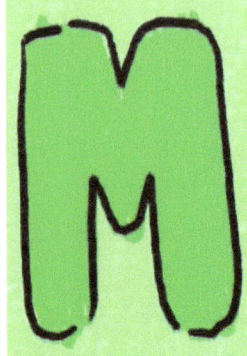

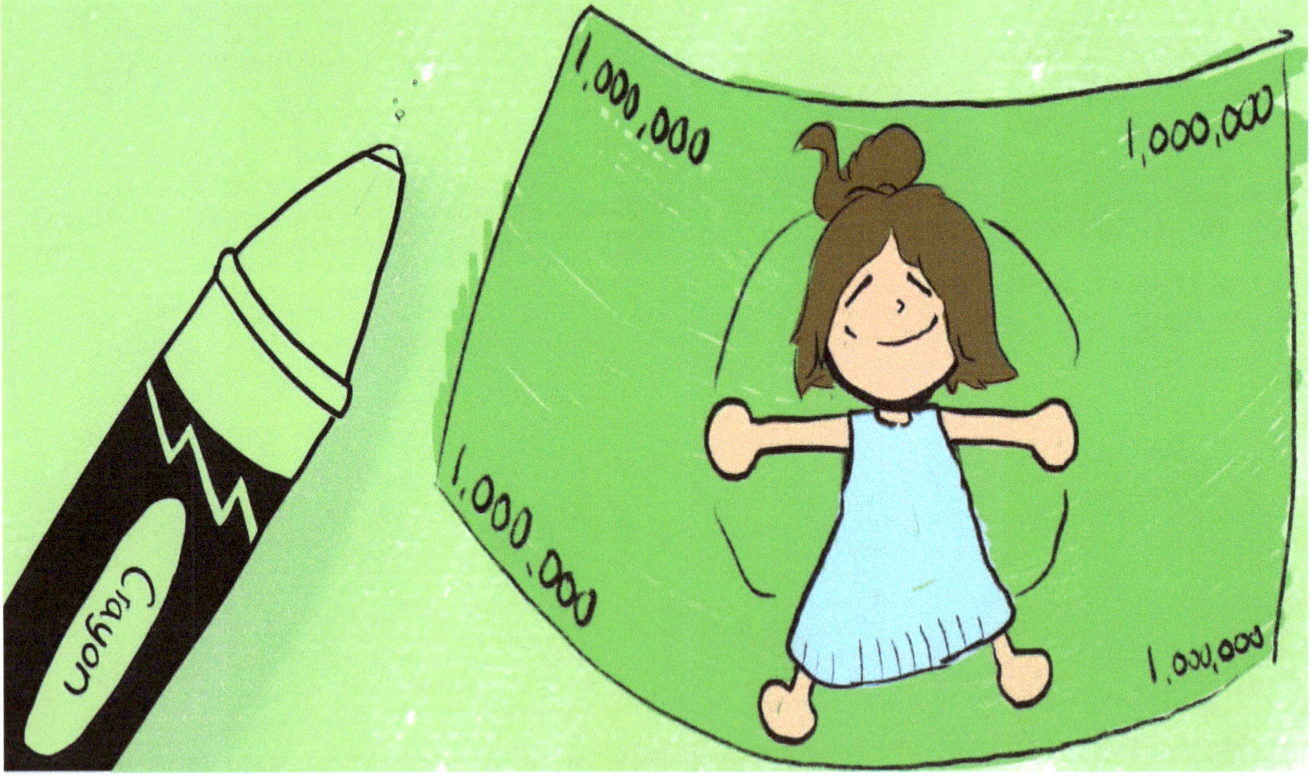

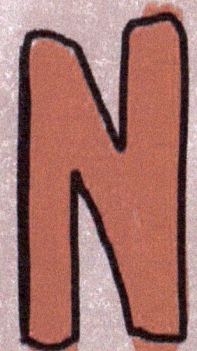 **Is for NETWORK**
(/net.werk/)

Get to know others.

 **Is for OWN**
(/on/)

When you own it, it's yours!

P Is for Property
(/pra.per.de/)

Become your own landlord!

 **Is for QUIT**
(/kwit/)

**Never give up!
Always follow through.**

R Is for RATE
(/rat/)

Seek the best interest rate for you.

S Is for SUCCESS
(/sek.ses/)

When you try your best in everything you do.

T Is for TIME
(/tim/)

Everything takes time.

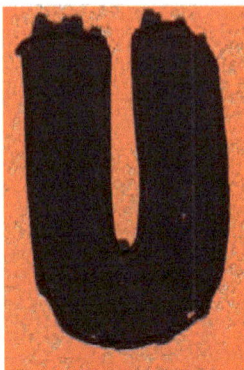 **Is for UNIVERSITY**
(/you.ne.versede/)

Higher learning for your mind.

V Is for VACATION
(/va.kash.en/)

Take trips and sip some lemonade in the shade.

W Is for WORLD
(/werld/)

Explore the world.
Don't be afraid!

Is for eXecute!
(/ekse.kyoot/)

Put in the work and make it happen!

You can do what you believe you can do.

Y Is all about YOU!
(/yoo/)

What God has for YOU, is for YOU!

When YOU take one step, God will take two.

Keep the faith and pray!

Z
Is for Zig Zag
(/zig.zag/)

Stay in your own lane and out the way!

GLOSSARY

Asset- property owned by a person or company, regarded as having value and available to meet debts, commitments, or legacies.

Business- a person's regular occupation, profession, or trade.

Credit- the ability of a customer to obtain goods or services before payment, based on the trust that payment will be made in the future.

Debt- something, typically money, that is owed or due.

Entrepreneur- a person who organizes and operates a business or businesses, taking on greater than normal financial risks to do so.

Finance- provide funding for (a person or enterprise).

Goals- the object of a person's ambition or effort; an aim or desired result.

Homeowner- a person who owns their own home.

Invest- provide or endow someone or something with (a particular quality or attribute).

Job- a paid position of regular employment.

Know- be aware of through observation, inquiry, or information.

Loan- a thing that is borrowed, especially a sum of money that is expected to be paid back with interest.

Money- a current medium of exchange in the form of coins and banknotes; coins and banknotes collectively.

Network- interact with others to exchange information and develop professional or social contacts.

Own- something that belongs to the person or thing mentioned.

Property- a thing or things belonging to someone; possessions collectively.

Quit- leave (a place), usually permanently, stop, evacuate.

Rate- a fixed price paid or charged for something, especially goods or services.

Success- the accomplishment of an aim or purpose.

Time- plan, schedule, or arrange when (something) should happen or be done.

University- an educational institution designed for instruction, examination, or both, of students in many branches of advanced learning, conferring degrees in various faculties, and often embodying colleges and similar institutions.

Vacation- an extended period of leisure and recreation, especially one spent away from home or in traveling.

World- the earth, together with all its countries, peoples, and natural features.

eXecute- carry out or put into effect (a plan, order, or course of action).

You- used to refer to the person or people that the speaker is addressing.

Zig-Zag- a line or course having abrupt alternate right and left turns.

www.ingramcontent.com/pod-product-compliance
Lightning Source LLC
Chambersburg PA
CBHW061116070526
44583CB00027B/3313